Even Still, Evolve Still: A Mood Calendar

Design by Mykel L. Brooks

Printed in the United States

ISBN: 978-1-7348285-1-1

Published in the United States by Evolving Still Publishing, a division of Evolving Still, LLC

Detroit, MI

www.evolvingstill.com

Evolving Still Publishing books are available at special discounts for bulk purchases for sales promotions or corporate use. Special editions, including personalized covers, excerpts of existing books, or books with corporate logos, can be created in large quantities for special needs. For more information, contact Evolving Still Publishing at contact@evolvingstill.com.

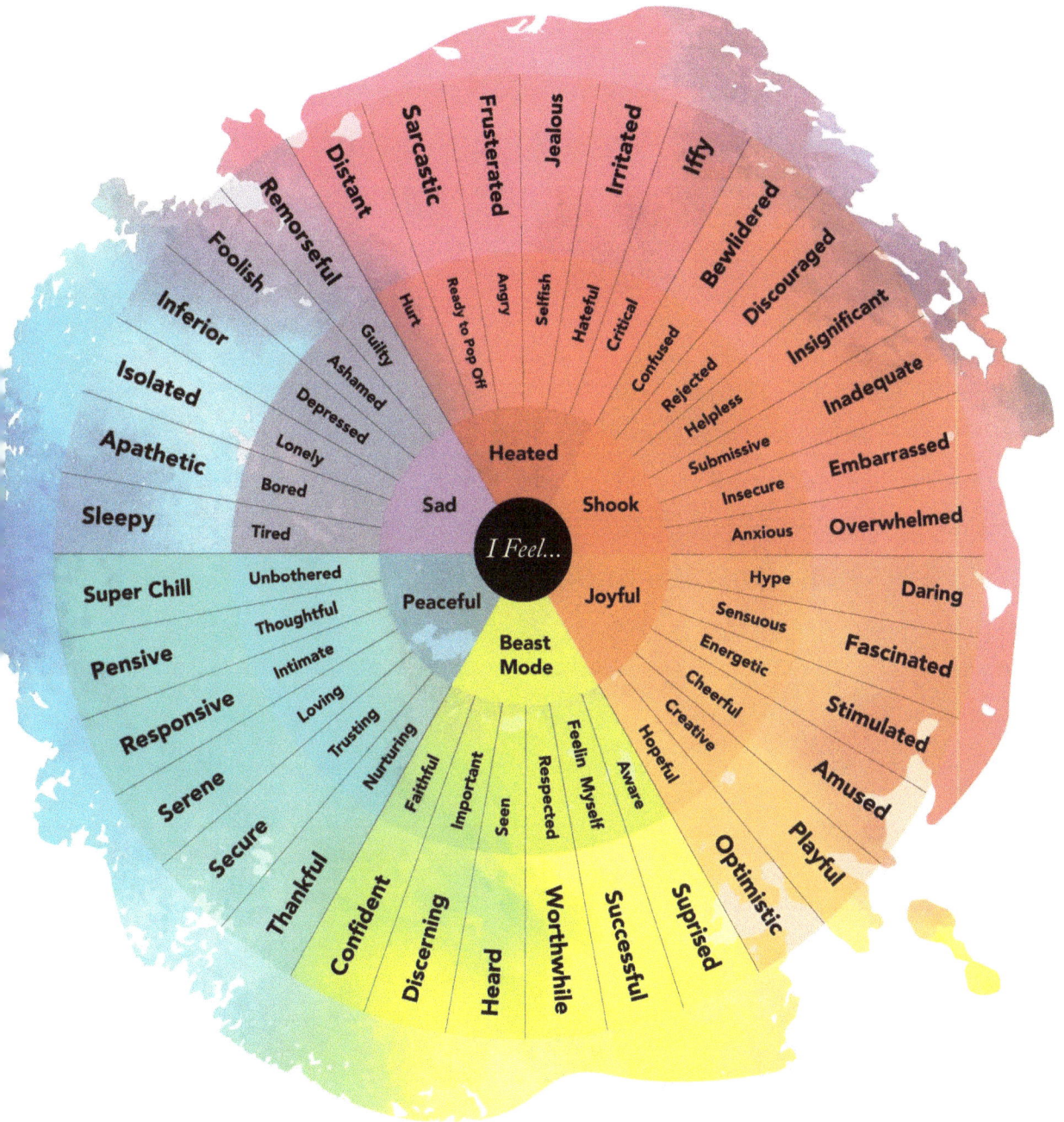

Inspired by Dr. Gloria Willcox

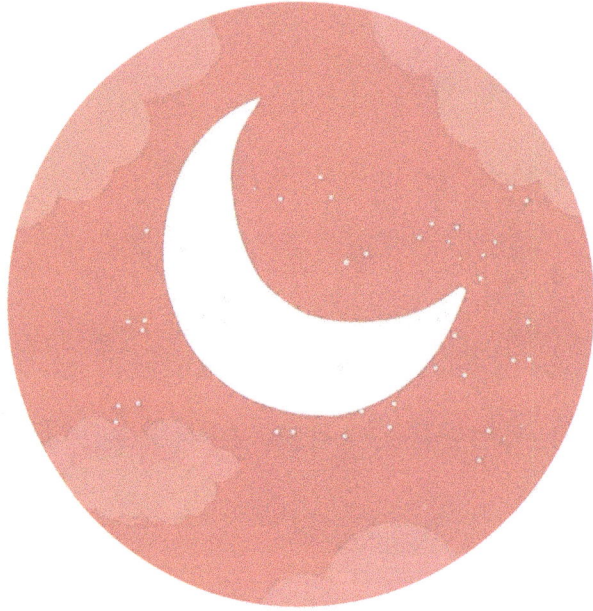

"The moon is a loyal companion. It never leaves. It's always there, watching, steadfast, knowing us in our light and dark moments, changing forever just as we do. Every day it's a different version of itself. Sometimes weak and wan, sometimes strong and full of light."

Letter from the Author,

First, I cannot describe how appreciative I am of your support. With this mood calendar being my second published project, I am just as (if not more) excited as I was when I released my first project-- the EDGE Guided Journal. I am extremely proud of this mood calendar because it was originally the idea that inspired the Evolving Still brand. The mood calendar is so special to me and I have been working so hard to give you guys a fully functional tool to use for 2024.

Tracking my moods is something that I found extremely helpful during my time in college. I was always very busy, and by filling out my mood calendar I was able to put a lot of things into perspective for myself. It helped me to realize that just because I had a bad day didn't always mean I would have a bad week. In a way, it gave me a reason to be intentional about the type of days I would have. If one bad thing happened I would be sure to do something that would balance it out. It almost became a game to me. After sharing on Instagram, other people also began to see the value in what I was doing and would ask me to show them how to track their moods too.

This mood calendar, like my guided journal, is extremely intentional. I have updated a few things to help make the calendar more functional. If you never used a mood calendar, here's how it works -- Step one: choose five colors. These colors are to represent your moods. For example, my favorite color is pink so that represents a great day in my calendar. Purple represents a good day. Blue represents an okay day. Green represents a stressful day. Red means I need to "Try again tomorrow." Step two: After choosing your colors, use the month's calendar to fill in the boxes according to your mood for each day. This time around, I added a few things like tasks and daily reflections to increase the functionality of the calendar. Step three: utilize the task column to plan out your day and the reflection column to reflect on how your day went! Additionally I added a space for you to choose a word to describe your day. If you want inspiration with describing your feelings check out the feelings wheel at the beginning of this journal to help you out. Though this is how I would suggest using the mood calendar this is your mindful tool so you should make it your own!

I hope you enjoy this calendar as much as I enjoyed creating it. I am super excited for you to use it and can't wait to hear your feedback. Hopefully, you can add this to your daily routine as we continue to evolve together.
Still Evolving,
Eboni

STILL Evolving

EBONI SAWYER

Creating Still Goals

When writing out goals be sure to make them STILL.
Specific, Timely, Introspective, Logical, and Lenient
What are Your Top Three Goals for the Year?

January

what's your mood today? *(choose a color)*

S	M	T	W	TH	F	S
	1	2	3	4	5	6
7	8	9	10	11	12	13
14	15	16	17	18	19	20
21	22	23	24	25	26	27
28	29	30	31			

weekly GOALS

M 1/1   Tasks   Reflections

○ _____   _____

○ _____   _____

                             _____

○ _____   _____

                             _____

○ _____   _____

word of the day

T 1/2   Tasks   Reflections

○ _____   _____

○ _____   _____

                             _____

○ _____   _____

                             _____

○ _____   _____

word of the day

W 1/3   Tasks   Reflections

○ _____   _____

○ _____   _____

                             _____

○ _____   _____

                             _____

○ _____   _____

word of the day

TH 1/4

Tasks   **Reflections**

○ ———————————   ———————————
○ ———————————   ———————————
                             ———————————
○ ———————————   ———————————
○ ———————————   ———————————

word of the day

F 1/5

Tasks   **Reflections**

○ ———————————   ———————————
○ ———————————   ———————————
                             ———————————
○ ———————————   ———————————
○ ———————————   ———————————

word of the day

SAT 1/6   ## SUN 1/7

———————————   ———————————
———————————   ———————————
———————————   ———————————
———————————   ———————————

M 1/8

Tasks   **Reflections**

○ _____   _____

○ _____   _____

○ _____   _____

○ _____   _____

word of the day

T 1/9

Tasks   **Reflections**

○ _____   _____

○ _____   _____

○ _____   _____

○ _____   _____

word of the day

W 1/10

Tasks   **Reflections**

○ _____   _____

○ _____   _____

○ _____   _____

○ _____   _____

word of the day

TH 1/11

Tasks	Reflections
○ ————————	————————
○ ————————	————————
○ ————————	————————
○ ————————	————————

word of the day

F 1/12

Tasks	Reflections
○ ————————	————————
○ ————————	————————
○ ————————	————————
○ ————————	————————

word of the day

SAT 1/13

———————————
———————————
———————————
———————————

SUN 1/14

———————————
———————————
———————————
———————————

M 1/15

Tasks | Reflections

O _____   _____

O _____   _____

O _____   _____

O _____   _____

word of the day

T 1/16

Tasks | Reflections

O _____   _____

O _____   _____

O _____   _____

O _____   _____

word of the day

W 1/17

Tasks | Reflections

O _____   _____

O _____   _____

O _____   _____

O _____   _____

word of the day

TH 1/18

Tasks	Reflections
○ _____	_____
○ _____	_____
○ _____	_____
○ _____	_____

word of the day

F 1/19

Tasks	Reflections
○ _____	_____
○ _____	_____
○ _____	_____
○ _____	_____

word of the day

SAT 1/20

_____

_____

_____

_____

SUN 1/21

_____

_____

_____

_____

weekly GOALS

M 1/22

Tasks   Reflections

○ ————————————   ————————————————

○ ————————————   ————————————————

                         ————————————————

○ ————————————   ————————————————

                         ————————————————

○ ————————————   ————————————————

word of the day

T 1/23

Tasks   Reflections

○ ————————————   ————————————————

○ ————————————   ————————————————

                         ————————————————

○ ————————————   ————————————————

                         ————————————————

○ ————————————   ————————————————

word of the day

W 1/24

Tasks   Reflections

○ ————————————   ————————————————

○ ————————————   ————————————————

                         ————————————————

○ ————————————   ————————————————

                         ————————————————

○ ————————————   ————————————————

word of the day

weekly GOALS

TH 1/25   Tasks   Reflections

○ _____   _____

○ _____   _____

○ _____   _____

○ _____   _____

          word of the day

F 1/26   Tasks   Reflections

○ _____   _____

○ _____   _____

○ _____   _____

○ _____   _____

          word of the day

SAT 1/27   SUN 1/28

_____   _____

_____   _____

_____   _____

_____   _____

weekly GOALS

M 1/29   **Tasks**   **Reflections**

○ _____   _____

○ _____   _____

○ _____   _____

○ _____   _____

word of the day

T 1/30   **Tasks**   **Reflections**

○ _____   _____

○ _____   _____

○ _____   _____

○ _____   _____

word of the day

W 1/31   **Tasks**   **Reflections**

○ _____   _____

○ _____   _____

○ _____   _____

○ _____   _____

word of the day

Goal Check-in

1. What are your current goals?

_____

_____

_____

_____

2. What steps do you need to take to achieve these goals?

_____

_____

_____

_____

"It is never too late to become what you might have been."

February

what's your mood today? *(choose a color)*

S	M	T	W	TH	F	S
				1	2	3
4	5	6	7	8	9	10
11	12	13	14	15	16	17
18	19	20	21	22	23	24
25	26	27	28	29		

Goal Check-in

1. What are your current goals?

_____

_____

_____

_____

2. What steps do you need to take to achieve these goals?

_____

_____

_____

_____

weekly GOALS

TH 2/1

Tasks | **Reflections**

○ _____

○ _____

○ _____

○ _____

word of the day

F 2/2

Tasks | **Reflections**

○ _____

○ _____

○ _____

○ _____

word of the day

SAT 2/3

SUN 2/4

M 2/5

Tasks   Reflections

○ _____   _____

○ _____   _____

○ _____   _____

○ _____   _____

word of the day

T 2/6

Tasks   Reflections

○ _____   _____

○ _____   _____

○ _____   _____

○ _____   _____

word of the day

W 2/7

Tasks   Reflections

○ _____   _____

○ _____   _____

○ _____   _____

○ _____   _____

word of the day

TH 2/8

Tasks	Reflections
○ _____	_____
○ _____	_____
○ _____	_____
○ _____	_____

word of the day

F 2/9

Tasks	Reflections
○ _____	_____
○ _____	_____
○ _____	_____
○ _____	_____

word of the day

SAT 2/10

_____

_____

_____

_____

SUN 2/11

_____

_____

_____

_____

weekly GOALS

M 2/12

Tasks   Reflections

○ _____   _____

○ _____   _____

○ _____   _____

○ _____   _____

word of the day

T 2/13

Tasks   Reflections

○ _____   _____

○ _____   _____

○ _____   _____

○ _____   _____

word of the day

W 2/14

Tasks   Reflections

○ _____   _____

○ _____   _____

○ _____   _____

○ _____   _____

word of the day

TH 2/15

Tasks   Reflections

○ _____   _____

○ _____   _____

                                  _____

○ _____   _____

                                  _____

○ _____   _____

word of the day

T 2/16

Tasks   Reflections

○ _____   _____

                                  _____

○ _____   _____

                                  _____

○ _____   _____

                                  _____

○ _____   _____

word of the day

SAT 2/17   ## SUN 2/18

_____   _____

_____   _____

_____   _____

_____   _____

_____   _____

weekly GOALS

M 2/19

Tasks

○ _____

○ _____

○ _____

○ _____

Reflections

_____

_____

_____

_____

word of the day

T 2/20

Tasks

○ _____

○ _____

○ _____

○ _____

Reflections

_____

_____

_____

_____

word of the day

W 2/21

Tasks

○ _____

○ _____

○ _____

○ _____

Reflections

_____

_____

_____

_____

word of the day

TH 2/22

Tasks	Reflections
○	
○	
○	
○	

word of the day

F 2/23

Tasks	Reflections
○	
○	
○	
○	

word of the day

SAT 2/24

SUN 2/25

M 2/26
Tasks   **Reflections**

○ _____

○ _____

○ _____

○ _____

word of the day

T 2/27
Tasks   **Reflections**

○ _____

○ _____

○ _____

○ _____

word of the day

W 2/28
Tasks   **Reflections**

○ _____

○ _____

○ _____

○ _____

word of the day

TH 2/29

Tasks

Reflections

○ _____

_____

○ _____

_____

_____

○ _____

_____

○ _____

_____

word of the day

F 3/1

Tasks

Reflections

○ _____

_____

○ _____

_____

_____

○ _____

_____

○ _____

_____

word of the day

SAT 3/2

SUN 3/3

Mindful Moment:

In what area of life do you need to practice patience and grace for yourself?

March

what's your mood today? *(choose a color)*

S	M	T	W	TH	F	S
					1	2
3	4	5	6	7	8	9
10	11	12	13	14	15	16
17	18	19	20	21	22	23
24	25	26	27	28	29	30
31						

Warm colors

Warm colors are often used to elicit strong emotional responses. Red, orange, and yellow are all associated with strong feelings.

Red is often thought to bring out emotions like passion, love, and power. It's attention-grabbing and can raise your pulse, which is why it's used in stop signs and other signals indicating caution or danger.

Yellow is associated with joy and optimism. It is often used to promote a sense of warmth and cheerfulness.

Orange is thought to combine the energy of red and happiness of yellow to evoke feelings of enthusiasm and creativity.

Cool colors

Cool colors like green, blue, and purple are often associated with a sense of calm, tranquility, and harmony.

Green is often linked to nature, growth, and renewal. It represents balance and harmony and has a calming effect on the eyes.

Blue is a color often associated with stability, depth, trust, and wisdom. It has a calming effect and is frequently used to convey a sense of reliability and security. Blue can also be associated with melancholy or even sadness.

Purple is a color that combines the energy of red and the stability of blue. It is often associated with creativity, luxury, and mystery. Historically, purple has been linked to royalty and power, and it continues to be associated with elegance and sophistication.

TH 2/29

Tasks	Reflections
○ _____	_____
○ _____	_____
○ _____	_____
○ _____	_____

word of the day

F 3/1

Tasks	Reflections
○ _____	_____
○ _____	_____
○ _____	_____
○ _____	_____

word of the day

SAT 3/2

_____

_____

_____

_____

SUN 3/3

_____

_____

_____

_____

weekly GOALS

M 3/4

Tasks   Reflections

- ⚪ _____   _____
- ⚪ _____   _____
- ⚪ _____   _____
- ⚪ _____   _____

word of the day

T 3/5

Tasks   Reflections

- ⚪ _____   _____
- ⚪ _____   _____
- ⚪ _____   _____
- ⚪ _____   _____

word of the day

W 3/6

Tasks   Reflections

- ⚪ _____   _____
- ⚪ _____   _____
- ⚪ _____   _____
- ⚪ _____   _____

word of the day

weekly GOALS

TH 3/7   **Tasks**   **Reflections**

○ ———————————————   ———————————————

○ ———————————————   ———————————————

○ ———————————————   ———————————————

○ ———————————————   ———————————————

word of the day

F 3/8   **Tasks**   **Reflections**

○ ———————————————   ———————————————

○ ———————————————   ———————————————

○ ———————————————   ———————————————

○ ———————————————   ———————————————

word of the day

SAT 3/9   **SUN 3/10**

————————————————   ————————————————

————————————————   ————————————————

————————————————   ————————————————

————————————————   ————————————————

weekly GOALS

M 3/11

Tasks   **Reflections**

○ _____   _____

○ _____   _____

○ _____   _____

○ _____   _____

word of the day

T 3/12

Tasks   **Reflections**

○ _____   _____

○ _____   _____

○ _____   _____

○ _____   _____

word of the day

W 3/13

Tasks   **Reflections**

○ _____   _____

○ _____   _____

○ _____   _____

○ _____   _____

word of the day

weekly GOALS

TH 3/14

Tasks	Reflections
○ _____	_____
○ _____	_____
○ _____	_____
○ _____	_____

word of the day

F 3/15

Tasks	Reflections
○ _____	_____
○ _____	_____
○ _____	_____
○ _____	_____

word of the day

SAT 3/16

_____

_____

_____

_____

SUN 3/17

_____

_____

_____

_____

weekly GOALS

M 3/18

Tasks   Reflections

○ —————————   ————————————
○ —————————   ————————————
                              ————————————
○ —————————   ————————————
                              ————————————
○ —————————   ————————————
word of the day

T 3/19

Tasks   Reflections

○ —————————   ————————————
○ —————————   ————————————
                              ————————————
○ —————————   ————————————
                              ————————————
○ —————————   ————————————
word of the day

W 3/20

Tasks   Reflections

○ —————————   ————————————
○ —————————   ————————————
                              ————————————
○ —————————   ————————————
                              ————————————
○ —————————   ————————————
word of the day

TH 3/21

Tasks	Reflections
○ _____	_____
○ _____	_____
○ _____	_____
○ _____	_____

word of the day

F 3/22

Tasks	Reflections
○ _____	_____
○ _____	_____
○ _____	_____
○ _____	_____

word of the day

SAT 3/23

_____
_____
_____
_____

SUN 3/24

_____
_____
_____
_____

weekly GOALS

M 3/25

Tasks   Reflections

○ _____   _____

○ _____   _____

○ _____   _____

○ _____   _____

word of the day

T 3/26

Tasks   Reflections

○ _____   _____

○ _____   _____

○ _____   _____

○ _____   _____

word of the day

W 3/27

Tasks   Reflections

○ _____   _____

○ _____   _____

○ _____   _____

○ _____   _____

word of the day

TH 3/28

Tasks	Reflections
○ _____	_____
○ _____	_____
○ _____	_____
○ _____	_____

word of the day

F 3/29

Tasks	Reflections
○ _____	_____
○ _____	_____
○ _____	_____
○ _____	_____

word of the day

SAT 3/30

_____

_____

_____

_____

SUN 3/31

_____

_____

_____

_____

"The secret to having it all is knowing you already do."

April

what's your mood today? *(choose a color)*

S	M	T	W	TH	F	S
	1	2	3	4	5	6
7	8	9	10	11	12	13
14	15	16	17	18	19	20
21	22	23	24	25	26	27
28	29	30				

weekly GOALS

M 4/1

Tasks	Reflections
○ _____	_____
○ _____	_____
○ _____	_____
○ _____	_____

word of the day

T 4/2

Tasks	Reflections
○ _____	_____
○ _____	_____
○ _____	_____
○ _____	_____

word of the day

W 4/3

Tasks	Reflections
○ _____	_____
○ _____	_____
○ _____	_____
○ _____	_____

word of the day

weekly GOALS

TH 4/4   Tasks   Reflections

-
-
-
-

word of the day

F 4/5   Tasks   Reflections

-
-
-
-

word of the day

SAT 4/6   SUN 4/7

M 4/8

	Tasks	Reflections
○	_____	_____
○	_____	_____
○	_____	_____
○	_____	_____

word of the day

T 4/9

	Tasks	Reflections
○	_____	_____
○	_____	_____
○	_____	_____
○	_____	_____

word of the day

W 4/10

	Tasks	Reflections
○	_____	_____
○	_____	_____
○	_____	_____
○	_____	_____

word of the day

TH 4/11

Tasks

○ _____

○ _____

○ _____

○ _____

word of the day

Reflections

_____

_____

_____

_____

F 4/12

Tasks

○ _____

○ _____

○ _____

○ _____

word of the day

Reflections

_____

_____

_____

_____

SAT 4/13

_____

_____

_____

_____

SUN 4/14

_____

_____

_____

_____

M 4/15　　　　　Tasks　　　　　Reflections

○ _____　　_____

○ _____　　_____

○ _____　　_____

○ _____　　_____

word of the day

T 4/16　　　　　Tasks　　　　　Reflections

○ _____　　_____

○ _____　　_____

○ _____　　_____

○ _____　　_____

word of the day

W 4/17　　　　　Tasks　　　　　Reflections

○ _____　　_____

○ _____　　_____

○ _____　　_____

○ _____　　_____

word of the day

TH 4/18

Tasks	Reflections
○	
○	
○	
○	

word of the day

F 4/19

Tasks	Reflections
○	
○	
○	
○	

word of the day

SAT 4/20

SUN 4/21

weekly GOALS

M 4/22   Tasks   Reflections

○ _____   _____

○ _____   _____

                             _____

○ _____   _____

                             _____

○ _____   _____

        word of the day

T 4/23   Tasks   Reflections

○ _____   _____

○ _____   _____

                             _____

○ _____   _____

                             _____

○ _____   _____

        word of the day

W 4/24   Tasks   Reflections

○ _____   _____

○ _____   _____

                             _____

○ _____   _____

                             _____

○ _____   _____

        word of the day

TH 4/25

Tasks	Reflections
○ _____	_____
○ _____	_____
○ _____	_____
○ _____	_____

word of the day

F 4/26

Tasks	Reflections
○ _____	_____
○ _____	_____
○ _____	_____
○ _____	_____

word of the day

SAT 4/27

_____

_____

_____

_____

SUN 4/28

_____

_____

_____

_____

weekly GOALS

M 4/29

Tasks | Reflections

○ _____
○ _____
○ _____
○ _____

word of the day

T 4/30

Tasks | Reflections

○ _____
○ _____
○ _____
○ _____

word of the day

W 5/1

Tasks | Reflections

○ _____
○ _____
○ _____
○ _____

word of the day

Goal Check-in

1. What are your current goals?

_____

_____

_____

_____

2. What steps do you need to take to achieve these goals?

_____

_____

_____

_____

Mindful Moment:

"Think back to the goals you set for yourself this year. How many have you accomplished thus far? Have you had to rethink any of your goals? What will it take for you to accomplish the remaining goals that you have set?

May

what's your mood today? *(choose a color)*

S	M	T	W	TH	F	S
			1	2	3	4
5	6	7	8	9	10	11
12	13	14	15	16	17	18
19	20	21	22	23	24	25
26	27	28	29	30	31	

M 4/29

Tasks	Reflections
○ _____	_____
○ _____	_____
○ _____	_____
○ _____	_____

word of the day

T 4/30

Tasks	Reflections
○ _____	_____
○ _____	_____
○ _____	_____
○ _____	_____

word of the day

W 5/1

Tasks	Reflections
○ _____	_____
○ _____	_____
○ _____	_____
○ _____	_____

word of the day

weekly GOALS

TH 5/2

Tasks	Reflections
○ _____	_____
○ _____	_____
○ _____	_____
○ _____	_____

word of the day

F 5/3

Tasks	Reflections
○ _____	_____
○ _____	_____
○ _____	_____
○ _____	_____

word of the day

SAT 5/4

SUN 5/5

weekly GOALS

M 5/6   Tasks   Reflections

O _____   _____

O _____   _____

O _____   _____

O _____   _____

word of the day

T 5/7   Tasks   Reflections

O _____   _____

O _____   _____

O _____   _____

O _____   _____

word of the day

W 5/8   Tasks   Reflections

O _____   _____

O _____   _____

O _____   _____

O _____   _____

word of the day

TH 5/9

Tasks

Reflections

- _____ _____
- _____ _____
  _____
- _____ _____
- _____ _____

word of the day

F 5/10

Tasks

Reflections

- _____ _____
- _____ _____
  _____
- _____ _____
- _____ _____

word of the day

SAT 5/11

SUN 5/12

weekly GOALS

M 5/13

Tasks

- ⚪ ———————————
- ⚪ ———————————
- ⚪ ———————————
- ⚪ ———————————

Reflections

word of the day

T 5/14

Tasks

- ⚪ ———————————
- ⚪ ———————————
- ⚪ ———————————
- ⚪ ———————————

Reflections

word of the day

W 5/15

Tasks

- ⚪ ———————————
- ⚪ ———————————
- ⚪ ———————————
- ⚪ ———————————

Reflections

word of the day

TH 5/16

Tasks	Reflections
⭘ _____	_____
⭘ _____	_____
	_____
⭘ _____	_____
⭘ _____	_____

word of the day

F 5/17

Tasks	Reflections
⭘ _____	_____
⭘ _____	_____
	_____
⭘ _____	_____
⭘ _____	_____

word of the day

SAT 5/18

_____

_____

_____

_____

SUN 5/19

_____

_____

_____

_____

weekly GOALS

M 5/20

Tasks   **Reflections**

○ _____   _____

○ _____   _____

                            _____

○ _____   _____

○ _____   _____

word of the day

T 5/21

Tasks   **Reflections**

○ _____   _____

○ _____   _____

                            _____

○ _____   _____

○ _____   _____

word of the day

W 5/22

Tasks   **Reflections**

○ _____   _____

○ _____   _____

                            _____

○ _____   _____

○ _____   _____

word of the day

TH 5/23

Tasks   **Reflections**

○ _____   _____

○ _____   _____

○ _____   _____

○ _____   _____

word of the day

F 5/24

Tasks   **Reflections**

○ _____   _____

○ _____   _____

○ _____   _____

○ _____   _____

word of the day

SAT 5/25

_____

_____

_____

_____

SUN 5/26

_____

_____

_____

_____

weekly GOALS

M 5/27   Tasks   Reflections

○ _____ _____

○ _____ _____

○ _____ _____

○ _____ _____

word of the day

T 5/28   Tasks   Reflections

○ _____ _____

○ _____ _____

○ _____ _____

○ _____ _____

word of the day

W 5/29   Tasks   Reflections

○ _____ _____

○ _____ _____

○ _____ _____

○ _____ _____

word of the day

TH 5/30

Tasks	Reflections
○ _____	_____
○ _____	_____
	_____
○ _____	_____
	_____
○ _____	_____

word of the day

F 5/31

Tasks	Reflections
○ _____	_____
○ _____	_____
	_____
○ _____	_____
	_____
○ _____	_____

word of the day

SAT 6/1

_____

_____

_____

_____

SUN 6/2

_____

_____

_____

_____

"If plan A didn't work, the alphabet has 25 more letters."

June

what's your mood today? *(choose a color)*

S	M	T	W	TH	F	S
						1
2	3	4	5	6	7	8
9	10	11	12	13	14	15
16	17	18	19	20	21	22
23	24	25	26	27	28	29
30						

Happy colors

Bright and warm shades, such as yellow, orange, pink, and red, are often associated with happiness, energy, and optimism. These colors can evoke feelings of warmth, excitement, and joy.

Pastel colors, such as peach, light pink, and lilac, are softer versions of these bright hues and are often perceived as calming and gentle, still eliciting feelings of happiness but in a more subtle and soothing

TH 5/30

Tasks   Reflections

- _____   _____
- _____   _____
                         _____
- _____   _____
                         _____
- _____   _____

word of the day

F 5/31

Tasks   Reflections

- _____   _____
- _____   _____
                         _____
- _____   _____
                         _____
- _____   _____

word of the day

SAT 6/1

_____
_____
_____
_____

SUN 6/2

_____
_____
_____
_____

weekly GOALS

M 6/3
Tasks

○ ———————————

○ ———————————

○ ———————————

○ ———————————

Reflections

word of the day

T 6/4
Tasks

○ ———————————

○ ———————————

○ ———————————

○ ———————————

Reflections

word of the day

W 6/5
Tasks

○ ———————————

○ ———————————

○ ———————————

○ ———————————

Reflections

word of the day

TH 6/6

Tasks	Reflections

○ _____

○ _____

○ _____

○ _____

word of the day

F 6/7

Tasks	Reflections

○ _____

○ _____

○ _____

○ _____

word of the day

SAT 6/8

_____

_____

_____

_____

SUN 6/9

_____

_____

_____

_____

M 6/10

Tasks   Reflections

○ ———————————

○ ———————————

○ ———————————

○ ———————————

word of the day

T 6/11

Tasks   Reflections

○ ———————————

○ ———————————

○ ———————————

○ ———————————

word of the day

W 6/12

Tasks   Reflections

○ ———————————

○ ———————————

○ ———————————

○ ———————————

word of the day

TH 6/13

Tasks	Reflections
○ _____	_____
○ _____	_____
○ _____	_____
○ _____	_____

word of the day

F 6/14

Tasks	Reflections
○ _____	_____
○ _____	_____
○ _____	_____
○ _____	_____

word of the day

SAT 6/15

_____

_____

_____

_____

SUN 6/16

_____

_____

_____

_____

weekly GOALS

M 6/17

Tasks

○ _____

○ _____

○ _____

○ _____

word of the day

Reflections

T 6/18

Tasks

○ _____

○ _____

○ _____

○ _____

word of the day

Reflections

W 6/19

Tasks

○ _____

○ _____

○ _____

○ _____

word of the day

Reflections

TH 6/20

Tasks	Reflections
○ _____	_____
○ _____	_____
○ _____	_____
○ _____	_____

word of the day

F 6/21

Tasks	Reflections
○ _____	_____
○ _____	_____
○ _____	_____
○ _____	_____

word of the day

SAT 6/22

_____

_____

_____

_____

SUN 6/23

_____

_____

_____

_____

M 6/24

Tasks   Reflections

○ _____   _____

○ _____   _____

○ _____   _____

○ _____   _____

word of the day

T 6/25

Tasks   Reflections

○ _____   _____

○ _____   _____

○ _____   _____

○ _____   _____

word of the day

W 6/26

Tasks   Reflections

○ _____   _____

○ _____   _____

○ _____   _____

○ _____   _____

word of the day

weekly GOALS

TH 6/27

Tasks	Reflections
○ _____	_____
○ _____	_____
○ _____	_____
○ _____	_____

word of the day

F 6/28

Tasks	Reflections
○ _____	_____
○ _____	_____
○ _____	_____
○ _____	_____

word of the day

SAT 6/29

_____

_____

_____

_____

SUN 6/30

_____

_____

_____

_____

Mindful Moment:

What goals have you set for yourself and accomplished this year?
What goals can you reframe?

July

what's your mood today? *(choose a color)*

S	M	T	W	TH	F	S
	1	2	3	4	5	6
7	8	9	10	11	12	13
14	15	16	17	18	19	20
21	22	23	24	25	26	27
28	29	30	31			

weekly GOALS

M 7/1

Tasks	Reflections
⭘ _____	_____
⭘ _____	_____
⭘ _____	_____
⭘ _____	_____

word of the day

T 7/2

Tasks	Reflections
⭘ _____	_____
⭘ _____	_____
⭘ _____	_____
⭘ _____	_____

word of the day

W 7/3

Tasks	Reflections
⭘ _____	_____
⭘ _____	_____
⭘ _____	_____
⭘ _____	_____

word of the day

weekly GOALS

TH 7/4   Tasks   Reflections

○ _____   _____
                                                    _____
○ _____   _____
                                                    _____
○ _____   _____
                                                    _____
○ _____   _____
                            word of the day   _____

F 7/5   Tasks   Reflections

○ _____   _____
                                                    _____
○ _____   _____
                                                    _____
○ _____   _____
                                                    _____
○ _____   _____
                            word of the day   _____

SAT 7/6   ## SUN 7/7

_____   _____

_____   _____

_____   _____

_____   _____

M 7/8

Tasks   Reflections

○ _____   _____
○ _____   _____
○ _____   _____
○ _____   _____

word of the day

T 7/9

Tasks   Reflections

○ _____   _____
○ _____   _____
○ _____   _____
○ _____   _____

word of the day

W 7/10

Tasks   Reflections

○ _____   _____
○ _____   _____
○ _____   _____
○ _____   _____

word of the day

TH 7/11

Tasks

Reflections

○ ————————————
○ ————————————
○ ————————————
○ ————————————

word of the day

F 7/12

Tasks

Reflections

○ ————————————
○ ————————————
○ ————————————
○ ————————————

word of the day

SAT 7/13

SUN 7/14

M 7/15

Tasks　　　　　　　Reflections

○ _____　_____

○ _____　_____

○ _____　_____

○ _____　_____

word of the day

T 7/16

Tasks　　　　　　　Reflections

○ _____　_____

○ _____　_____

○ _____　_____

○ _____　_____

word of the day

W 7/17

Tasks　　　　　　　Reflections

○ _____　_____

○ _____　_____

○ _____　_____

○ _____　_____

word of the day

TH 7/18

Tasks	Reflections
○ _____	_____
○ _____	_____
○ _____	_____
○ _____	_____

word of the day

F 7/19

Tasks	Reflections
○ _____	_____
○ _____	_____
○ _____	_____
○ _____	_____

word of the day

SAT 7/20

_____

_____

_____

_____

SUN 7/21

_____

_____

_____

_____

weekly GOALS

M 7/22

Tasks   **Reflections**

○ ——————————   ——————————

○ ——————————   ——————————

○ ——————————   ——————————

○ ——————————   ——————————

word of the day

T 7/23

Tasks   **Reflections**

○ ——————————   ——————————

○ ——————————   ——————————

○ ——————————   ——————————

○ ——————————   ——————————

word of the day

W 7/24

Tasks   **Reflections**

○ ——————————   ——————————

○ ——————————   ——————————

○ ——————————   ——————————

○ ——————————   ——————————

word of the day

TH 7/25

Tasks	Reflections
○ _____	_____
○ _____	_____
○ _____	_____
○ _____	_____

word of the day

F 7/26

Tasks	Reflections
○ _____	_____
○ _____	_____
○ _____	_____

word of the day

SAT 7/27

_____

_____

_____

_____

SUN 7/28

_____

_____

_____

_____

M 7/29

Tasks   Reflections

○ _____   _____

○ _____   _____

○ _____   _____

○ _____   _____

word of the day

T 7/30

Tasks   Reflections

○ _____   _____

○ _____   _____

○ _____   _____

○ _____   _____

word of the day

W 7/31

Tasks   Reflections

○ _____   _____

○ _____   _____

○ _____   _____

○ _____   _____

word of the day

Goal Check-in

1. What are your current goals?

_____

_____

_____

_____

2. What steps do you need to take to achieve these goals?

_____

_____

_____

_____

"You wanna fly, you have to give up the sh*t that weighs you down"

- Toni Morrison

August

what's your mood today? *(choose a color)*

S	M	T	W	TH	F	S
				1	2	3
4	5	6	7	8	9	10
11	12	13	14	15	16	17
18	19	20	21	22	23	24
25	26	27	28	29	30	31

Sad colors

Sad colors are often associated with darker, muted, and neutral tones, which can convey feelings of somberness, melancholy, or even mourning. Colors like gray, brown, and beige are neutral and lack the vibrancy associated with happier or more energetic colors. These muted tones can create a sense of dullness or sadness.

Certain shades of blue and green can also be perceived as sad, especially darker or cooler versions of these colors.

In Western cultures, black is commonly associated with mourning and grief. It symbolizes a sense of loss and is often worn at funerals or memorial services. In some East Asian countries, white is the color of mourning. White is associated with purity and simplicity, and in this context, it represents the transition from life to death.

weekly GOALS

TH 8/1

Tasks	Reflections

○ _____

○ _____

○ _____

○ _____

word of the day

F 8/2

Tasks	Reflections

○ _____

○ _____

○ _____

○ _____

word of the day

SAT 8/3

SUN 8/4

weekly GOALS

M 8/5   Tasks   Reflections

○ ——————————————   ——————————————

○ ——————————————   ——————————————

○ ——————————————   ——————————————

○ ——————————————   ——————————————

word of the day

T 8/6   Tasks   Reflections

○ ——————————————   ——————————————

○ ——————————————   ——————————————

○ ——————————————   ——————————————

○ ——————————————   ——————————————

word of the day

W 8/7   Tasks   Reflections

○ ——————————————   ——————————————

○ ——————————————   ——————————————

○ ——————————————   ——————————————

○ ——————————————   ——————————————

word of the day

TH 8/8   Tasks   Reflections

○ _____   _____
○ _____   _____
                          _____
○ _____   _____
                          _____
○ _____   _____

word of the day

T 8/9   Tasks   Reflections

○ _____   _____
○ _____   _____
                          _____
○ _____   _____
                          _____
○ _____   _____

word of the day

SAT 8/10   SUN 8/11

_____   _____

_____   _____

_____   _____

_____   _____

M 8/12

Tasks **Reflections**

○ _____ _____

○ _____ _____

○ _____ _____

○ _____ _____

word of the day

T 8/13

Tasks **Reflections**

○ _____ _____

○ _____ _____

○ _____ _____

○ _____ _____

word of the day

W 8/14

Tasks **Reflections**

○ _____ _____

○ _____ _____

○ _____ _____

○ _____ _____

word of the day

weekly GOALS

TH 8/15   Tasks   Reflections

○ _____
○ _____
○ _____
○ _____

word of the day

F 8/16   Tasks   Reflections

○ _____
○ _____
○ _____
○ _____

word of the day

SAT 8/17   SUN 8/18

weekly GOALS

M 8/19

Tasks

- ⚪ _____
- ⚪ _____
- ⚪ _____
- ⚪ _____

Reflections

word of the day

T 8/20

Tasks

- ⚪ _____
- ⚪ _____
- ⚪ _____
- ⚪ _____

Reflections

word of the day

W 8/21

Tasks

- ⚪ _____
- ⚪ _____
- ⚪ _____
- ⚪ _____

Reflections

word of the day

- weekly GOALS

TH 8/22   **Tasks**   **Reflections**

○ _____ _____

○ _____ _____

○ _____ _____

○ _____ _____

word of the day

F 8/23   **Tasks**   **Reflections**

○ _____ _____

○ _____ _____

○ _____ _____

○ _____ _____

word of the day

SAT 8/24   SUN 8/25

weekly GOALS

M 8/26   **Tasks**   **Reflections**

○ ———————————   ———————————

○ ———————————   ———————————

○ ———————————   ———————————

○ ———————————   ———————————

word of the day

T 8/27   **Tasks**   **Reflections**

○ ———————————   ———————————

○ ———————————   ———————————

○ ———————————   ———————————

○ ———————————   ———————————

word of the day

W 8/28   **Tasks**   **Reflections**

○ ———————————   ———————————

○ ———————————   ———————————

○ ———————————   ———————————

○ ———————————   ———————————

word of the day

weekly GOALS

TH 8/29   **Tasks**   **Reflections**

○ _____

○ _____

○ _____

○ _____

word of the day

F 8/30   **Tasks**   **Reflections**

○ _____

○ _____

○ _____

○ _____

word of the day

SAT 8/31   SUN 9/1

Mindful Moment:

"How different are your current goals from the ones you set at the beginning of the year?

September

what's your mood today? *(choose a color)*

S	M	T	W	TH	F	S
1	2	3	4	5	6	7
8	9	10	11	12	13	14
15	16	17	18	19	20	21
22	23	24	25	26	27	28
29	30					

Goal Check-in

1. What are your current goals?

_____

_____

_____

_____

2. What steps do you need to take to achieve these goals?

_____

_____

_____

_____

TH 8/29

Tasks	Reflections
○ _____	_____
	_____
○ _____	_____
	_____
○ _____	_____
	_____
○ _____	_____

word of the day

F 8/30

Tasks	Reflections
○ _____	_____
	_____
○ _____	_____
	_____
○ _____	_____
	_____
○ _____	_____

word of the day

SAT 8/31

_____

_____

_____

_____

SUN 9/1

_____

_____

_____

_____

weekly GOALS

M 9/2   Tasks   Reflections

○ _____   _____

○ _____   _____

○ _____   _____

○ _____   _____

word of the day

T 9/3   Tasks   Reflections

○ _____   _____

○ _____   _____

○ _____   _____

○ _____   _____

word of the day

W 9/4   Tasks   Reflections

○ _____   _____

○ _____   _____

○ _____   _____

○ _____   _____

word of the day

TH 9/5

Tasks	Reflections
○ ———————	———————
○ ———————	———————
○ ———————	———————
○ ———————	———————

word of the day

F 9/6

Tasks	Reflections
○ ———————	———————
○ ———————	———————
○ ———————	———————
○ ———————	———————

word of the day

SAT 9/7

—————————
—————————
—————————
—————————

SUN 9/8

—————————
—————————
—————————
—————————

weekly GOALS

M 9/9   Tasks   Reflections

○ _____

○ _____

○ _____

○ _____

word of the day

T 9/10   Tasks   Reflections

○ _____

○ _____

○ _____

○ _____

word of the day

W 9/11   Tasks   Reflections

○ _____

○ _____

○ _____

○ _____

word of the day

weekly GOALS

TH 9/12

Tasks	Reflections
○ _____	_____
○ _____	_____
○ _____	_____
○ _____	_____

word of the day

F 9/13

Tasks	Reflections
○ _____	_____
○ _____	_____
○ _____	_____
○ _____	_____

word of the day

SAT 9/14

_____

_____

_____

_____

SUN 9/15

_____

_____

_____

_____

M 9/16

Tasks	Reflections
○ ——————————	——————————
○ ——————————	——————————
○ ——————————	——————————
○ ——————————	——————————

word of the day

T 9/17

Tasks	Reflections
○ ——————————	——————————
○ ——————————	——————————
○ ——————————	——————————
○ ——————————	——————————

word of the day

W 9/18

Tasks	Reflections
○ ——————————	——————————
○ ——————————	——————————
○ ——————————	——————————
○ ——————————	——————————

word of the day

TH 9/19

Tasks | Reflections

⭕ _____ _____

⭕ _____ _____

⭕ _____ _____

⭕ _____ _____

word of the day

F 9/20

Tasks | Reflections

⭕ _____ _____

⭕ _____ _____

⭕ _____ _____

⭕ _____ _____

word of the day

SAT 9/21

_____

_____

_____

_____

SUN 9/22

_____

_____

_____

_____

M 9/23

Tasks | Reflections

○ ————————————— ————————————————

○ ————————————— ————————————————

○ ————————————— ————————————————

○ ————————————— ————————————————

word of the day

T 9/24

Tasks | Reflections

○ ————————————— ————————————————

○ ————————————— ————————————————

○ ————————————— ————————————————

○ ————————————— ————————————————

word of the day

W 9/25

Tasks | Reflections

○ ————————————— ————————————————

○ ————————————— ————————————————

○ ————————————— ————————————————

○ ————————————— ————————————————

word of the day

weekly GOALS

TH 9/26

Tasks	Reflections
○ ___	___
○ ___	___
○ ___	___
○ ___	___

word of the day

F 9/27

Tasks	Reflections
○ ___	___
○ ___	___
○ ___	___
○ ___	___

word of the day

SAT 9/28

SUN 9/29

weekly GOALS

M 9/30 Tasks Reflections

○ _____ _____

○ _____ _____

○ _____ _____

○ _____ _____

word of the day

T 10/1 Tasks Reflections

○ _____ _____

○ _____ _____

○ _____ _____

○ _____ _____

word of the day

W 10/2 Tasks Reflections

○ _____ _____

○ _____ _____

○ _____ _____

○ _____ _____

word of the day

Calming colors

Turning to cool colors like blue and green, as well as their pastel variations such as baby blue, lilac, and mint, can create a calming and soothing atmosphere. These colors are often associated with nature, water, and the sky, evoking feelings of tranquility and relaxation.

Neutral tones like white and gray provide a subtle and understated backdrop, creating a sense of simplicity and serenity. When there are fewer colors competing for attention, it can reduce visual clutter and promote a feeling of clarity and calm.

"It always seems impossible until it's done"

- Nelson Mandela

October

what's your mood today? *(choose a color)*

S	M	T	W	TH	F	S
		1	2	3	4	5
6	7	8	9	10	11	12
13	14	15	16	17	18	19
20	21	22	23	24	25	26
27	28	29	30	31		

weekly GOALS

M 9/30   Tasks   Reflections

○ ——————————

○ ——————————

○ ——————————

○ ——————————

word of the day

T 10/1   Tasks   Reflections

○ ——————————

○ ——————————

○ ——————————

○ ——————————

word of the day

W 10/2   Tasks   Reflections

○ ——————————

○ ——————————

○ ——————————

○ ——————————

word of the day

weekly GOALS

TH 10/3　　　Tasks　　　Reflections

○ ———————————　———————————

○ ———————————　———————————

○ ———————————　———————————

○ ———————————　———————————

word of the day

F 10/4　　　Tasks　　　Reflections

○ ———————————　———————————

○ ———————————　———————————

○ ———————————　———————————

word of the day

SAT 10/5　　　　　　SUN 10/6

M 10/7

Tasks | Reflections

○ _____

○ _____

○ _____

○ _____

word of the day

T 10/8

Tasks | Reflections

○ _____

○ _____

○ _____

○ _____

word of the day

W 10/9

Tasks | Reflections

○ _____

○ _____

○ _____

○ _____

word of the day

weekly GOALS

TH 10/10

Tasks · Reflections

○ _____
○ _____
○ _____
○ _____

word of the day

F 10/11

Tasks · Reflections

○ _____
○ _____
○ _____
○ _____

word of the day

SAT 10/12

SUN 10/13

weekly GOALS

M 10/14

Tasks   Reflections

○ _____   _____

○ _____   _____

○ _____   _____

○ _____   _____

word of the day

T 10/15

Tasks   Reflections

○ _____   _____

○ _____   _____

○ _____   _____

○ _____   _____

word of the day

W 10/16

Tasks   Reflections

○ _____   _____

○ _____   _____

○ _____   _____

○ _____   _____

word of the day

weekly GOALS

TH 10/17   Tasks   Reflections

- ○ _____   _____
- ○ _____   _____
                       _____
- ○ _____   _____
- ○ _____   _____

word of the day

F 10/18   Tasks   Reflections

- ○ _____   _____
- ○ _____   _____
                       _____
- ○ _____   _____
- ○ _____   _____

word of the day

SAT 10/19   SUN 10/20

M 10/21

Tasks

Reflections

○ ——————————

○ ——————————

○ ——————————

○ ——————————

word of the day

T 10/22

Tasks

Reflections

○ ——————————

○ ——————————

○ ——————————

○ ——————————

word of the day

W 10/23

Tasks

Reflections

○ ——————————

○ ——————————

○ ——————————

○ ——————————

word of the day

TH 10/24

Tasks

Reflections

- _____
- _____
- _____
- _____

word of the day

F 10/25

Tasks

Reflections

- _____
- _____
- _____
- _____

word of the day

SAT 10/26

_____

_____

_____

_____

SUN 10/27

_____

_____

_____

_____

weekly GOALS

M 10/28

Tasks

Reflections

○ _____

_____

○ _____

_____

○ _____

_____

○ _____

_____

word of the day

T 10/29

Tasks

Reflections

○ _____

_____

○ _____

_____

○ _____

_____

○ _____

_____

word of the day

W 10/30

Tasks

Reflections

○ _____

_____

○ _____

_____

○ _____

_____

○ _____

_____

word of the day

weekly GOALS

TH 10/31

Tasks

Reflections

○ _____
○ _____
○ _____
○ _____

word of the day

F 11/1

Tasks

Reflections

○ _____
○ _____
○ _____
○ _____

word of the day

SAT 11/2

_____
_____
_____
_____
_____

SUN 11/3

_____
_____
_____
_____
_____

Mindful Moment:

What are your top 5 lessons from this year?

November

what's your mood today? *(choose a color)*

S	M	T	W	TH	F	S
					1	2
3	4	5	6	7	8	9
10	11	12	13	14	15	16
17	18	19	20	21	22	23
24	25	26	27	28	29	30

Goal Check-in

1. What are your current goals?

_____

_____

_____

_____

2. What steps do you need to take to achieve these goals?

_____

_____

_____

_____

TH 10/1

Tasks | Reflections

○ _____

○ _____

○ _____

○ _____

word of the day

F 11/1

Tasks | **Reflections**

○ _____

○ _____

○ _____

○ _____

word of the day

SAT 11/2

_____

_____

_____

_____

SUN 11/3

_____

_____

_____

_____

weekly GOALS

M 11/4   Tasks   Reflections

○ ——————————   ——————————————

○ ——————————   ——————————————

                                    ——————————————

○ ——————————   ——————————————

○ ——————————   ——————————————
          word of the day

T 11/5   Tasks   Reflections

○ ——————————   ——————————————

○ ——————————   ——————————————

○ ——————————   ——————————————

○ ——————————   ——————————————
          word of the day

W 11/6   Tasks   Reflections

○ ——————————   ——————————————

○ ——————————   ——————————————

○ ——————————   ——————————————

○ ——————————   ——————————————
          word of the day

TH 11/7

Tasks	Reflections
⭕ _____	_____
⭕ _____	_____
⭕ _____	_____
⭕ _____	_____

word of the day

F 11/8

Tasks	Reflections
⭕ _____	_____
⭕ _____	_____
⭕ _____	_____
⭕ _____	_____

word of the day

SAT 11/9

_____

_____

_____

_____

SUN 11/10

_____

_____

_____

_____

weekly GOALS

M 11/11

Tasks   Reflections

○ ———————————   ———————————

○ ———————————   ———————————

○ ———————————   ———————————

○ ———————————   ———————————

word of the day

T 11/12

Tasks   Reflections

○ ———————————   ———————————

○ ———————————   ———————————

○ ———————————   ———————————

○ ———————————   ———————————

word of the day

W 11/13

Tasks   Reflections

○ ———————————   ———————————

○ ———————————   ———————————

○ ———————————   ———————————

○ ———————————   ———————————

word of the day

TH 11/14

Tasks   Reflections

○ _____   _____

○ _____   _____

                         _____

○ _____   _____

○ _____   _____

word of the day

F 11/15

Tasks   Reflections

○ _____   _____

○ _____   _____

                         _____

○ _____   _____

○ _____   _____

word of the day

SAT 11/16   SUN 11/17

_____   _____

_____   _____

_____   _____

_____   _____

_____   _____

weekly GOALS

M 11/18   **Tasks**   **Reflections**

O _____ _____

O _____ _____

O _____ _____

O _____ _____

word of the day

T 11/19   **Tasks**   **Reflections**

O _____ _____

O _____ _____

O _____ _____

O _____ _____

word of the day

W 11/20   **Tasks**   **Reflections**

O _____ _____

O _____ _____

O _____ _____

O _____ _____

word of the day

TH 11/21

Tasks	Reflections
○ _____	_____
○ _____	_____
	_____
○ _____	_____
	_____
○ _____	_____

word of the day

F 11/22

Tasks	Reflections
○ _____	_____
○ _____	_____
	_____
○ _____	_____
	_____
○ _____	_____

word of the day

SAT 11/23

_____

_____

_____

_____

SUN 11/24

_____

_____

_____

_____

weekly GOALS

M 11/25   Tasks   Reflections

○ ————————————   ————————————————
○ ————————————   ————————————————
                                               ————————————————
○ ————————————   ————————————————
                                               ————————————————
○ ————————————   ————————————————
          word of the day

T 11/26   Tasks   Reflections

○ ————————————   ————————————————
○ ————————————   ————————————————
                                               ————————————————
○ ————————————   ————————————————
                                               ————————————————
○ ————————————   ————————————————
          word of the day

W 11/27   Tasks   Reflections

○ ————————————   ————————————————
○ ————————————   ————————————————
                                               ————————————————
○ ————————————   ————————————————
                                               ————————————————
○ ————————————   ————————————————
          word of the day

weekly GOALS

TH 11/28   Tasks   Reflections

○ _____   _____

○ _____   _____

                                   _____

○ _____   _____

○ _____   _____

word of the day

F 11/29   Tasks   Reflections

○ _____   _____

○ _____   _____

                                     _____

○ _____   _____

○ _____   _____

word of the day

SAT 11/30   SUN 12/1

_____   _____

_____   _____

_____   _____

_____   _____

"Year's end is neither an end nor a beginning, but a going on with all the wisdom that experience has instilled in us."

December

what's your mood today? *(choose a color)*

S	M	T	W	TH	F	S
1	2	3	4	5	6	7
8	9	10	11	12	13	14
15	16	17	18	19	20	21
22	23	24	25	26	27	28
29	30	31				

Energizing colors

Bright and highly saturated colors like bright red, yellow, neon green, turquoise, magenta, and emerald green can have a powerful impact on our emotions, often evoking feelings of excitement, energy, and enthusiasm

These colors are vibrant and visually stimulating, and they tend to stand out prominently from their surroundings. Their boldness and intensity make us feel more energetic, passionate, and fired up.

TH 11/28

Tasks	Reflections

word of the day

F 11/29

Tasks	Reflections

word of the day

SAT 11/30

SUN 12/1

weekly GOALS

M 12/2

Tasks	Reflections
○ ———————	———————
○ ———————	———————
○ ———————	———————
○ ———————	———————

word of the day

T 12/3

Tasks	Reflections
○ ———————	———————
○ ———————	———————
○ ———————	———————
○ ———————	———————

word of the day

W 12/4

Tasks	Reflections
○ ———————	———————
○ ———————	———————
○ ———————	———————
○ ———————	———————

word of the day

TH 12/5

Tasks	Reflections
○ _____	_____
○ _____	_____
○ _____	_____
○ _____	_____

word of the day

F 12/6

Tasks	Reflections
○ _____	_____
○ _____	_____
○ _____	_____
○ _____	_____

word of the day

SAT 12/7

_____

_____

_____

_____

SUN 12/8

_____

_____

_____

_____

weekly GOALS

M 12/9   Tasks   Reflections

○ ——————————   ——————————————

○ ——————————   ——————————————

○ ——————————   ——————————————

○ ——————————   ——————————————

word of the day

T 12/10   Tasks   Reflections

○ ——————————   ——————————————

○ ——————————   ——————————————

○ ——————————   ——————————————

○ ——————————   ——————————————

word of the day

W 12/11   Tasks   Reflections

○ ——————————   ——————————————

○ ——————————   ——————————————

○ ——————————   ——————————————

○ ——————————   ——————————————

word of the day

TH 12/12

Tasks	Reflections
○ _____	_____
○ _____	_____
○ _____	_____
○ _____	_____

word of the day

F 12/13

Tasks	Reflections
○ _____	_____
○ _____	_____
○ _____	_____
○ _____	_____

word of the day

SAT 12/14

_____

_____

_____

_____

SUN 12/15

_____

_____

_____

_____

weekly GOALS

M 12/16

Tasks   Reflections

○ _____   _____

○ _____   _____

○ _____   _____

○ _____   _____

word of the day

T 12/17

Tasks   Reflections

○ _____   _____

○ _____   _____

○ _____   _____

○ _____   _____

word of the day

W 12/18

Tasks   Reflections

○ _____   _____

○ _____   _____

○ _____   _____

○ _____   _____

word of the day

TH 12/19

Tasks	Reflections
○ _____	_____
○ _____	_____
○ _____	_____
○ _____	_____

word of the day

F 12/20

Tasks	Reflections
○ _____	_____
○ _____	_____
○ _____	_____
○ _____	_____

word of the day

SAT 12/21

_____

_____

_____

_____

SUN 12/22

_____

_____

_____

_____

weekly GOALS

M 12/23
Tasks   Reflections

○ _____

○ _____

○ _____

○ _____

word of the day

T 12/24
Tasks   Reflections

○ _____

○ _____

○ _____

○ _____

word of the day

W 12/25
Tasks   Reflections

○ _____

○ _____

○ _____

○ _____

word of the day

weekly GOALS

TH 12/26

Tasks   Reflections

○ _____   _____
○ _____   _____
                      _____
○ _____   _____
○ _____   _____

word of the day

F 12/27

Tasks   Reflections

○ _____   _____
○ _____   _____
                      _____
○ _____   _____
○ _____   _____

word of the day

SAT 12/28   ## SUN 12/29

_____   _____
_____   _____
_____   _____
_____   _____

M 12/30

Tasks   Reflections

○ ——————————   ——————————

○ ——————————   ——————————

○ ——————————   ——————————

○ ——————————   ——————————

word of the day

T 12/31

Tasks   Reflections

○ ——————————   ——————————

○ ——————————   ——————————

○ ——————————   ——————————

○ ——————————   ——————————

word of the day

W 1/1

Tasks   Reflections

○ ——————————   ——————————

○ ——————————   ——————————

○ ——————————   ——————————

○ ——————————   ——————————

word of the day

"Whether you accomplished every goal you set this year or changed your Top Three multiple times, this calendar is a reminder that like the moon we are all evolving, still."

-Eboni Sawyer

www.ingramcontent.com/pod-product-compliance
Lightning Source LLC
Chambersburg PA
CBHW060755150426
42811CB00058B/1419